Time Management

Effective Time Management: Conquer Procrastination And Minimize Time Waste - Strategies For Optimizing Your Time And Enhancing Productivity

(Strategies For Overcoming Chronic Lateness, Embracing Timeliness, And Maintaining Punctuality)

Armando Winters

TABLE OF CONTNET

Methodical Organizing 1

Dividing Objectives Into Doable Steps 8

A Beneficial Effect On Your Health 20

Eisenhower Matrix Hierarchy Of Needs 37

Organize Your Time 53

Setting Priorities And Making Plans 76

Conventional Instruments For Monitoring Goals ... 96

Tenacity To Dispel Myths 124

The Significance Of Proficient Time Management. 148

Methodical Organizing

The Value of Organization

One essential instrument for efficient time management is strategic planning.

It enables you to identify your objectives, create targets, and arrange your work to use your time and resources as efficiently as possible.

We'll look at methods and strategies in this chapter to assist you in developing a successful strategic plan.

Setting Strategic Objectives

Establishing specific targets that complement your long-term objectives is the first stage in strategic planning.

The following tactics can assist you in establishing strategic goals:

Long-Term Objectives: Determine your goals over a longer period, such as a year, three, or five years.

Set challenging objectives that will motivate and propel your career and personal development.

Short-Term Objectives: Divide your long-term objectives into shorter, more manageable targets.

These intermediate objectives give a sense of accomplishment and progress by acting as checkpoints along the route.

Metas SMART: Make sure your objectives are clearly stated and focused on achieving observable outcomes using the SMART (specific, measurable, achievable, relevant, and time-bound) method.

Methods of Planning

You may maximize your time and manage your tasks with various planning strategies.

The following are a few of the best methods:

List of Tasks: Make a to-do list that is weekly, monthly, or daily.

Sort your jobs according to priority and urgency.

Mark the completion of each task as you finish it. This aids in tracking your development and maintaining focus.

Eisenhower Matrix: Once more, divide your jobs into four categories according to their urgency and priority using the

Eisenhower matrix discussed in the previous chapter.

This makes it easier to determine which jobs should be completed right once and which ones may wait or be assigned.

Weekly Planning: Schedule your tasks and top priorities for the next few days at the start of each week.

This helps you focus and clarify at the beginning of the week by letting you know what must be done first.

Calendar and Agenda:

Use a planner or calendar to arrange crucial meetings, appointments, and deadlines.

Doing this lets you see how much time you have open and prevent schedule problems.

Adjustments and Flexibility

While preparation is crucial, being adaptable and willing to make changes is also critical.

Situations might alter, bringing with them unanticipated priorities and new needs.

The following advice can help you deal with the requirement for adjustments:

Additional Time Booking: Allow time in your schedule for unanticipated events and last-minute tasks.

An unplanned window of time keeps you from feeling overwhelmed and stressed.

Continual Evaluation: Review your plan occasionally and make any necessary revisions.

This will enable you to modify your plan to keep it current and relevant.

Interrupt Management: Create plans for handling diversions and interruptions that are inevitable. Keep an eye on your schedule and, if needed, establish firm boundaries.

Ongoing Evaluation and Education

Once your plan has been implemented, assessing its success and drawing lessons from the process is critical. Here's how to go about doing it:

Analysis of the results: Review your progress against set targets regularly. Determine what was successful and what needed improvement.

Utilize this knowledge to enhance your future planning.

Input and Self-Assessment: To get outside views on your performance and planned strategy, ask leaders, mentors, or peers for their input.

Additionally, evaluate yourself honestly to find areas where you can develop and improve.

Ongoing Education:

Keep an open mind and be willing to try new planning strategies and tactics.

The art of efficient time management is a never-ending process, and you can improve your abilities by learning more.

After finishing this chapter, you will be well-equipped with strategic planning approaches to make the most use of your time and resources.

Recall that efficient planning is a continuous process that calls for adaptability and adjustments as necessary.

Continue reading for the following chapter, where we'll look at organizing strategies to help you manage your time better.

Dividing Objectives Into Doable Steps

It entails dissecting your ambitious ambitions into more achievable, smaller actions that will move you closer to your ultimate aims. The following procedures can be used to divide objectives into doable tasks:

1. Begin with your grander objectives: Decide your overarching aims or objectives first. You may wish to accomplish these as short-term or long-term goals. Divide your bigger objective, such as launching a new product, into smaller ones.

2. Determine the essential tasks: Determine the jobs or endeavors essential to achieving your main objectives. These must be precise, doable actions that advance your main objective. For instance, designing the product, developing a marketing strategy, and carrying out market

research can all be essential if your objective is to introduce a new product.

3. Set task priorities: After determining the essential tasks, order them according to significance and urgency. This aids in keeping your attention on the most important activities to reach your objective.

4. Divide jobs into smaller chunks: Divide each activity into smaller, easier-to-manage chunks. They become less scary and more bearable as a result. If your objective is to perform market research, divide it into smaller tasks like determining your target market, developing a survey, and assessing the results.

5. Establish deadlines: Set deadlines for each activity or subtask to help you remain on track and progress closer to your objective.

6. Monitor progress: Pay careful attention to how you're doing while you work toward your goals and responsibilities. This facilitates your ability to stick to and adjust your plan as needed.

If your main objective is to introduce a new product, for instance, you may divide it up into smaller goals like these:

* Perform market research; two-week deadline
- Determine your target market (one week is the deadline).

- Make a survey; two days are the deadline.
- Conduct data analysis (due in one week)

* Design product (one-month deadline)
- Study materials (two-week deal deadline)
- Mockups must be created by the end of three weeks.

* Draft a marketing strategy before the end of two weeks.
- Designate channels (with a one-week deadline).
- Crafting messaging (within a week)

Conclusively, dividing objectives into feasible jobs is crucial in proficient time management. You can progress toward marketing and success by beginning with bigger goals, determining necessary activities, prioritizing tasks, splitting projects into smaller portions, setting linens, and keeping track of progress.

Setting Priorities for Your Objectives

Setting priorities for your objectives is essential to efficient time management. It entails determining which objectives are most essential to you and allocating time and energy to complete them. To assist you in prioritizing your goals, consider the following steps:

1. List all your objectives: List everything you wish to accomplish first. These could be long-term or short-term, professional or personal, or any other objectives that are significant to you.

2. Assess every objective: Next, rank each aim according to its significance, immediacy, and applicability. Consider the following: • How important is this objective to me?

• Can this aim be accomplished at any time, or is there a deadline?

• In what way does this objective fit into my larger vision and mission?

3. Organize your objectives: Divide your objectives into three categories: high, medium, and low priority. Goals classified as high-priority are the most crucial and urgent, medium-priority are significant but less urgent, and low-priority are less critical and may wait till later.

4. Concentrate on high-priority objectives: Give your time and energy to accomplish your top priorities first. This will guarantee that you are attending to the most pressing needs first and assist you in moving closer to your most critical goals.

5. Strike a balance between medium- and low-priority goals: Prioritizing high-priority goals is vital, but you should also allocate enough time and resources to medium- and low-priority goals. This will enable you to prioritize your most crucial goals while still moving closer to these goals.

6. Review and modify your priorities: Review and reassess your priorities

regularly in light of evolving circumstances, ambitions, and life events. This will assist you in staying on course and guarantee that you are moving closer to your most crucial goals. For instance, if your objectives are to: • Introduce a new product (high priority)

• Enhance customer support (mid priority)

• Acquire a low-priority new skill.

Due to its high priority and immediacy, you would direct your time and resources toward launching a new product first. Then, since acquiring a new skill and enhancing customer service are both medium- and low-priority objectives, you would divide your time and resources between them.

In summary, setting priorities for your objectives is essential to efficient time management. You can move closer to your most significant Creatives and chapter success by creating a list of all your objectives, assessing each, classifying your goals, concentrating on high-priority goals, striking a balance between medium- and low-priority goals, and routinely analyzing and revising your priorities.

Including Adaptability in Your Timetable
Having some flexibility in your schedule is essential to efficient time management. It's crucial to set and follow a timetable, but it's also critical to be adaptable and flexible in the face of

unforeseen circumstances or schedule adjustments. Adaptability can be included in your schedule in the following ways:

1. Allow extra time for emergencies or delays when creating your timetable. This can help you avoid feeling hurried or upset if anything unexpected happens.

2. Make time for breaks: Plan your day to include breaks that will help you refuel and prevent burnout.

3. Be flexible: Have backup plans if something unforeseen arises. You can avoid tension and frustration by doing this and maintaining your adaptability.

4. Develop the ability to say "no": Avoid taking on too much by refusing to accept

every invitation or request. Set priorities for your responsibilities and tasks, and practice saying "no" to requests that conflict with your principles or aspirations.

5. Have reasonable expectations: Avoid cramming too much into your schedule or having irrational ideas about how much you can get done in a day. Stress and exhaustion may result from this. Rather, establish reasonable goals for both your calendar and yourself.

Adding flexibility to your calendar will help you accomplish your objectives, feel less stressed and frustrated, and better manage your time. You may make a plan that works for you and enables you to be successful by being flexible and allowing for breaks and buffer time.

A Beneficial Effect On Your Health

The effects of working from home on your physical and emotional well-being can be profound:

You'll have more energy and be able to exercise and engage in other activities.

You'll discover you're eating healthier because hunting for snacks at work in the afternoon is simple when you're feeling low on energy. To avoid temptations, consider healthy snacks and eliminate junk food from your household.

You won't always be exhausted, and your thoughts of work won't be clouded by negativity, which will lift your spirits.

Fewer sick days will result from leading a healthy lifestyle.

You feel satisfied when you realize how well everything fits together.

We all want to be happy, and living a balanced, healthy lifestyle helps us achieve this.

As you can see, working from home has benefits and drawbacks. Nonetheless, more people are choosing to work from home due to the above advantages. They have, like me, discovered strategies to eradicate the drawbacks and change their perspectives so they do not encounter them. We shall go to this next. You, too, may enjoy working from home and reap all these benefits by following these six simple steps. Making your workstation is the initial step in the entire process.

Chapter 2: Set Up Your Desk

Setting up a workspace is the first step toward managing a home office. If you don't have a spare room or study, it doesn't have to be a fully functional home office. All you need is a special workplace place that will resemble a workplace and help you get in the appropriate frame of mind. So, all it will take to know when to start working is to go into your office. Knowing what to put in your workspace makes it easy to set up. It goes beyond simply the furnishings and apparatuses. You need to consider software, stationary, and the setup's impact on your house. Having extension cords running through busy parts of the house is a recipe for trouble, and while having a home phone may appear convenient, keeping track of the many expenses may be challenging.

A home office needs to be carefully considered. If your house lacks a designated office space, you should pick a peaceful location where you won't be readily distracted. For instance, if your family spends most of their time in the dining room or living room setting up your workplace, that is not a smart idea. Keeping things distinct will assist you in maintaining attention. A workstation is more than just a place to put your laptop and connect to the internet. Because an office plan is pre-established when we start our work, we frequently fail to recognize the amount of thought that goes into it. You'll learn from working from home that there are several necessities to make your life at work more convenient.

Considerations for Organizing a Workspace

I've compiled a list of necessities for a home office or workspace in this section. It is more important to emphasize the needs that will have the most influence than it is to go out and buy a ton of goods. These make up the foundation of a quality workspace.

Choosing the Proper Location

I mentioned this before, but let's specify where you should shop for your workstation. First, using a covered balcony, study, guest room, or garage as an office is a terrific idea. You can create the necessary divide between your living and working rooms by installing a door between these busy areas. Because your family will be less likely to enter your office as they know you are working, you won't become sidetracked once you enter and shut the door.

If you don't have a spare room, you'll need to locate a specific area to set up your office. In this case, you should stay away from residential locations where you know your family hangs out during the day. The sound of the kitchen blender or a television should not divert your attention. You also don't want to interfere with your family's regular schedule. It's equally annoying to have them remain silent, so you may hold an online conference as it is to have them interrupt you.

You should still arrange your workstation in a distraction-free area, even if you live alone. Windows can be a source of comfort as well as diversion. Thus, if you'd like to be close to a window, pick wisely and stay away from windows that face a busy street. Choose a location where your desk, chair, and other office supplies will fit comfortably. Make sure you can move around a little and have enough plug points. The worst thing you can do is arrange your workstation so that you have to squeeze into a small, dim area. Instead of detesting your office, you should love it!

Honor yourself—you deserve it!

Every time your child accomplishes anything exceptional, it's worth celebrating. Acknowledging their achievements with pride is essential for their motivation and self-worth.

But it's also critical to acknowledge and be proud of your accomplishments as a single mother.

Your path as a single mother is paved with setbacks and victories. It's critical to recognize and rejoice in these accomplishments, no matter how tiny. This is why it matters:

● Increasing self-assurance: Reminding yourself of your ability and bolstering your self-confidence are two benefits of celebrating your successes. It serves as a strong incentive to keep going.

● Setting a good example: You may teach your kids the value of self-worth and self-appreciation by acknowledging and celebrating your accomplishments. You serve as an example of positive self-esteem.

● Acknowledging patience: Your resilience is demonstrated by your ability to handle the challenges of being a single parent. Honoring your path demonstrates your resilience and strength.

● Promoting an optimistic atmosphere: Festivities in your house produce an optimistic and upbeat attitude. They provide opportunities for happiness, camaraderie, and introspection on your accomplishments.

You can commemorate your own and your kids' accomplishments in several ways, some of which are included below:

● Positive reinforcement: Use positive reinforcement to congratulate your youngster on their achievements. Honor their efforts and draw attention to their development.

● Personal milestones: Assign specific goals for yourself and your child. Celebrate these accomplishments with one another when they are reached. It might be finishing a task, getting a good grade, or getting beyond a difficulty.

● Festivities with family: Plan unique family get-togethers to commemorate noteworthy accomplishments. These get-togethers foster lifelong memories and emphasize the value of community.

● Self-care routines: Celebrate yourself by indulging in self-care rituals. This may be treating yourself to a favorite dish, a spa day, or a beloved hobby.

- Expressing appreciation: Give thanks for your experience and the advancements you've achieved. Keep a gratitude notebook to help you remember the good things in your life.

Honoring accomplishments—your own or your child's—helps to create a supportive and caring atmosphere. It builds resilience, self-worth, and a feeling of achievement.

Furthermore, it supports the notion that success involves acknowledging the work and progress made along the route in addition to the final objective.

Celebrating your accomplishments as a single mother is a great way to improve your self-worth, set an example of good behavior for your kids, and foster a loving atmosphere at home. It's a confirmation that your efforts are impacting and acknowledging how far along you've come in life.

Thus, rejoice, feel pleased with yourself, and keep going forward with assurance and optimism.

Chapter 2: Time Management Strategies' Foundations

Examining Typical Techniques

In today's society, time management techniques and tactics can be found in many different contexts, from personal to professional. Understanding standard practices gives us a base to construct unique, efficient time management methods.

Some of the most often used time management techniques are as follows:

List of things to do: It's among the easiest and most popular methods. It entails making a list of the things that need to be done. Having a clear idea of what has to be done is made easier with the help of this list, which is updated daily. A sense of completion can also be attained by the gratification of checking off or marking a work as completed.

The Pareto Principle, or 80/20 Rule: According to this theory, 20% of efforts yield 80% of the results. This suggests, in terms of time management, that a significant portion of the overall return can be obtained with a short amount of time spent on the appropriate task. The most crucial jobs should be identified and prioritized, as encouraged by this method.

The batching technique saves time and energy by grouping and scheduling related operations to be completed simultaneously. This eliminates the need to switch between jobs. It is especially handy when you have many little related jobs to complete.

Time Blocking Technique: It breaks the day into time blocks and allocates each block to a particular activity. Using this technique, one can avoid multitasking and make sure that each work receives adequate time.

Assignment of Tasks: One of the most crucial time management techniques, particularly for managers and leaders, is delegation. It entails delegating some duties to others to free up time for more important or high-priority tasks.

The Three Day Technique states that you should schedule a task to be completed within the next three days if you cannot execute it immediately when it is assigned. This keeps things from piling up and preserves efficient time management.

These are only a handful of the widely used time management techniques; there are many more, and custom solutions usually combine a number of them to meet the person's demands. While some people may discover that a combination of methods works best for them, others may find that one technique works better.

Understanding these techniques can lay a strong basis for increasing productivity and time management. It's crucial to remember that time management is not a precise science, and what functions for one person might not for another. Consequently, it's critical to test various tactics and determine which suits each person the best.

Eisenhower Matrix Hierarchy Of Needs

The foundation of efficient time management is prioritization. It entails determining which jobs or endeavors are the most crucial and ought to be completed first to make the most use of your limited time and energy. Without setting priorities, you can always find yourself responding to less important but urgent issues. This can cause stress, inefficiency, and a lack of progress toward your objectives.

Eisenhower was renowned for his outstanding time management abilities. The matrix is a straightforward yet incredibly powerful tool for dividing jobs into four groups according to their significance and urgency.

Important and Urgent (Quadrant I): This quadrant contains critical and urgent tasks. They should be given priority and must be attended to immediately. If these assignments are not completed on time, there might be serious repercussions, including deadlines, emergencies, or crises.

Quadrant II's "Important but Not Urgent" Tasks are crucial for achieving your long-term goals and objectives but aren't always time-sensitive. Completing these duties, which call for planning, is essential to reaching your biggest successes. Strategic planning, skill development, and relationship building are a few examples.

Quadrant III: Urgent but Not Important: Although the tasks in this quadrant are urgent, they don't significantly impact your long-term objectives or priorities. They are frequent disruptions or diversions that, if not handled carefully, can take up your time. These tasks must be minimized or delegated to free up time for more important things.

They should be cut back on or removed from your calendar because they are time wasters. This includes using social media excessively, aimlessly browsing the web and attending pointless meetings.

The Eisenhower Matrix is a useful tool when deciding how best to divide your time and energy. It assists you in concentrating on Quadrant II, where you should allocate a large amount of your time because they are the jobs necessary for personal growth and long-term success. You can increase your productivity and prioritize tasks consistent with your values and goals by limiting Quadrants III and IV and making the most effort to address Quadrant I.

A powerful storm tore through the community one day, destroying and wreaking extensive damage. Without delay, Ava assisted her fellow peasants in reconstructing their houses and livelihoods. She put in endless effort, day and night, to aid in the recovery of her neighborhood.

Ava never lost sight of the significance of self-care, even in the face of the daunting task at her. She was careful to take pauses and practice self-care whenever she could. She understood that she would be better positioned to care for others if she cared for herself.

The town recovered and rebuilt because of Ava's unrelenting devotion to self-care. The people in Ava's community knew they could always rely on her for support and direction and would always be thankful to her.

Everyone who knew Ava saw her as an inspiration for self-care after that day.

People traveled from far and wide to learn from her wisdom.

The conclusion.

It's crucial to understand that the narrative is made up and not based on any actual person or circumstance. The narrative merely served to illustrate how self-care may be incorporated into daily life and how it can improve one's well-being and the well-being of people around them.

Although it's not always simple, discipline is necessary to take control of our bodies. We may get the desired level of physical mastery by establishing a specific objective, creating a strategy, and persistently working toward it. We can change our physical appearance and enhance our general health through discipline, perseverance, and overcoming obstacles. Discipline allows us to control our body and reach our full potential."

The Advantages of Time Management Skills

As our previous exercises have shown, we probably have some free time and a skill set that will help us create distinctive organizing habits. It's also probable that you're eager to get going, and that's fantastic! To slightly sweeten the pot, though, here are a few advantages you will soon experience.

The positive feedback loop between time management productivity and happiness has already been discussed. However, this is more than that. Misra and McKean's (2000) research indicates that time management can reduce stress more successfully than recreational activities. However, this is not to say that you shouldn't engage in soothing activities. Their research found that a considerable reduction in stress can be achieved by combining anxiety control, leisure, and excellent time management.

Additionally, knowing exactly what must be done at any given time is advantageous. As we'll go into more detail in Chapter 2, this will represent your priorities. These can (and ought to) direct our time allocation. Including passion-driven activities in your calendar is usually smart because they help you balance your time between productive and leisurely pursuits.

Furthermore, we create room for the people we care about when we prioritize the things we truly believe in. We can also use some of our enhanced communication skills when interacting with them socially. This makes it possible for everyone to have clear expectations. We also have more time for the pastimes we think we're too busy for. There are innumerable anonymous surveys asking people what they would do if they had more time. Two common responses are those who would finally learn German or spend more time with their kids. Some people simply want some alone time, a book, and tea.

Someone even promised to install solar panels in his backyard so he could use them for an additional fifteen minutes daily! These hopes, meanwhile, seem unrealistic because time cannot be mass-produced in this way.

However, a lot of these idealists have disregarded effective time management. If these goals are significant enough to each individual, then anybody can achieve them. An amazing capacity to prioritize what is worthwhile and what just doesn't come from this. Time management does clear up our calendar. Everybody has encountered the idea that we should only keep possessions that make us happy to maintain a neat home. The same concept holds for managing your time well, even though life is typically more complex. Increase the activities that bring you joy. Expand on the things you are talented at. There's never enough time for everything. So why not exert all of our efforts?

We'll work together to expand on your priorities in the upcoming chapter. A clear vision of our destination will greatly aid our journey there. We'll also go over how to apply the SMART methodology for goal-setting and how it directly relates to optimizing our time. After classifying our outstanding chores using the Eisenhower Matrix and the Pareto Principle, we'll discuss how to monitor our progress and make necessary adjustments to our goals.

Chapter 5: Achieving Success in Procrastination

Plan of action: Use these strategies to quit procrastinating and boost productivity.

Procrastination is the silent productivity killer that impacts people in all spheres of life. Everyone has been guilty of procrastinating important tasks and seeing precious time slip away. So don't be alarmed! We cover much ground in the pamphlet "Procrastination No More," including overcoming procrastination and unlocking your potential. We'll implement a comprehensive strategy to eliminate procrastination and increase your output.

How to Resolve the Mysteries of Procrastination

Examine the psychology of putting things off.

Acknowledge the different types of procrastinators and the things that usually trigger them.

The Cost of Procrastination

Consider the unintended consequences of chronic procrastination.

Understand the impact on your goals, well-being, and overall standard of living.

How to Break the Procrastination Cycle

Identify the routines that promote procrastination.

Learn how to interrupt these patterns and establish new, productive ones.

Knowing Oneself Is Power

Become acutely aware of how you procrastinate.

Apply self-awareness to implement customized transformation strategies.

Methods for Completing Tasks

Discover how to beat procrastination with a collection of tried-and-true techniques.

Inspiration and Objective Establishment

Decide on clear, motivating goals that will motivate you to act.

Reward yourself and visualize your goals to stay on course.

Acknowledge the relationship between perfectionism and procrastination.

Recognize your flaws and accept that growth is more important than perfection.

the Distraction Dragon is in check

Acknowledge the origins of your daily distractions.

Employ strategies to lessen or eliminate these distractions.

Effective Time Management

Gain proficiency in time management to prevent procrastinating.

Gain knowledge of time management techniques to increase output.

Make strategies for getting back on track when you start putting things off.

Organize Your Time

Setting Task Priorities

For some businesses, more than others, the capacity to select and finish activities in the order of significance is desirable and demanding.

You need to be as aware of as many projects and responsibilities as possible before you can choose tasks. To do this, there must be a list at every planning session.

A List Is Essential!

After you have enumerated all your assignments, rank them and relist them in order. After that, you may schedule them. After rating every job and project, prioritize using the following extra filters:

- Consider the effects of doing away with the task. Many unnecessary duties will be eliminated after this practice.
- Select the best time to do each task: prime or secondary.
- Ascertain who the work will impact.

Right now, Cut Down on Your List

Most of us need to lighten our workload until we can successfully clone ourselves to be in multiple places simultaneously. Think about the following task reduction criteria before you begin to prioritize:

Does This Project or Task Make Sense?

You should have to initially meet this standard for every work you complete.

You have priorities, objectives, and goals. Does each task advance your overall goal? After estimating the time needed for each assignment, consider what you would do with the extra time if it weren't assigned. Even though it's not always feasible, everything you do should advance your goals.

How come the task is urgent?

While business should prioritize haste, urgency should also be relentlessly questioned. Is the hurry just to please other people? What is the reason behind the urgency? Innumerable urgent situations have resulted from errors. Finding the reason for the urgency might help you avoid or postpone a task and take preventative action against errors and disruptions.

Certain seemingly essential chores are not that urgent at all. Customers may be putting forth needless requests.

Consult with every one of the parties.

The Qualifying Delegation

Are you the only one qualified to complete the task? You may be at times, but there are plenty of situations when someone else can intervene. To clear your schedule, assign as much as you can.

How Else Might the Assignment Be Completed?

Do You Make Use of Technology?

Could a phone call replace an in-person appointment?

Conference calling can save travel and result in significant time savings.

Would you please email rather than call? Emailing can be done whenever and however you like.

You will have more time to speak clearly than a live phone discussion. Leaving phone messages for individuals can waste time and reduce sales. Phone tag is eliminated using email.

Is the Task Dissectable?

Can any tasks be rescheduled, cut down on, or delayed?

How Much Does It Cost to Remove a Task?

Throughout the day, numerous tasks are simply not worth the time invested. An additional way to gauge the worth of a task is to apply a monetary value when contemplating task cancellation.

The Task Value Measures

Cash: What is the task's estimated value?

Time: What is the expected duration?

Effect: Task Completed versus Task Cancelled Effectiveness: Which completion method yields the best results?

Contribution to Your Goals

Substitute: (How may the time be better used?)

Division: Breaking the Work Up Into Components

When: Is there a moment when a secondary performance of the activity is possible?

Setting deadlines for each work is an excellent way to prioritize.

3. The Head's Function in Time Management

How to Create a Productive Team and Lead by Example.

In addition to overseeing your schedule, time management as a business owner entails inspiring and guiding your staff to reach their greatest potential. In this chapter, we'll talk about the importance of leadership in time management and how to set a positive example for your team and foster productivity.

1. Set a good example

The foundation of efficient time management is leadership. A leader must set an example for the behaviors they desire from their team members. This entails exhibiting efficient time management techniques, such as meeting on time, setting priorities for your most important work, and assigning duties to others.

2. Express Your Expectations Evidently

Having clear communication is essential to time management success. Assign projects with precise due dates and give regular feedback to ensure everyone works toward the same goals.

3. Offer Guidance and Assistance

Not every team member will possess the same proficiency in managing their time. Give your team members the guidance and assistance they need to acquire the required time management skills. This could be one-on-one coaching, time management seminars, or access to tools and applications for productivity.

4. Honor and Commend Achievements

Time management that works takes work and commitment. Acknowledge and honor team members who accomplish their goals and show effective time management. This might foster a positive work atmosphere and inspire your staff.

5. Encourage a Productivity Culture

Establishing a productive culture helps support your team's motivation and attention. Promote cooperation and teamwork, and commemorate victories together as a group. Establish hard but attainable objectives and monitor advancement often to ensure everyone moves in the right direction.

6. Promote a balanced work-life

as increasing productivity at work when it comes to effective time management. Urge your team members to prioritize their mental health, take well-deserved breaks, and strike a healthy work-life balance. Increased productivity and job satisfaction may result from this.

Actual Cases:

1. Set a Good Example: As a business owner, you can set a good example for your employees by managing your time well. To show your team how to manage their time well, you might assign duties to others, prioritize your tasks wisely, and show up on time for meetings.

2. Express Your Expectations Clearly: To make sure your team members are aware of their duties and deadlines, you can express your expectations to them clearly and concisely. To make sure everyone is on track, you can, for instance, assign assignments with deadlines, give verbal or written directions, and schedule frequent check-ins.

3. Offer Training and assistance: To assist your team members in acquiring time management skills, you can offer them Training and assistance. For instance, you may hold time management seminars, give out tools or applications for productivity, and give team members who require more support one-on-one coaching.

4. Acknowledge and Honor Achievements: You can honor team members with excellent time management skills and accomplish their objectives. For example, you can inspire and uplift others by publicly praising team members' achievements, giving

verbal or written praise, or providing incentives or awards.

5. Promote a Productive Culture: You may encourage a productive culture in your group or company. To build a productive work atmosphere, you might, for instance, reward cooperation and teamwork, set ambitious but attainable goals, monitor progress frequently, and celebrate victories as a group.

6. Promote Work-Life Balance: You may motivate the people on your team to keep a positive work-life balance. To guarantee that team members have time for their personal lives, you might, for instance, prioritize mental health and well-being, encourage breaks during the workday, provide flexible work

schedules, and set boundaries. All of these actions can boost productivity and job satisfaction.

Steer Clear of Time Traps

Excellent executives and business owners can teach their staff various time management techniques. However, having authority over others simplifies slipping into time-wasting traps. The main time management issues that contractors deal with are listed here, along with some advice on how to completely avoid them.

1. Make wise delegations

As a brand-new company owner years ago, I faced the greatest fear of all entrepreneurs: delegation. It was difficult for me to envision giving up control to others and letting them handle things without my constant supervision. I was trying to micromanage every task at every level, which meant I had too much work to complete.

However, everything came to a head one morning when almost everything began to fail at once, and I understood for the first time that "my way" was preventing my firm from reaching its full potential as a place where employees could grow and learn alongside the business.

In the Harvard Business Review, Art Markman writes, "How to Stop Delegating and Start Teaching," which suggests that delegation should involve training and crossing tasks off your to-do list. If you delegate in a hurry because you can't finish a task or have a business flight to catch, you're setting your staff up for failure because they won't know how to work without you.

They eventually lose motivation and play it safe since they've had enough of those tiny setbacks. Even worse, assignments completed incorrectly are often the result of assigning work to unqualified individuals. In actuality, assigning work to unqualified individuals frequently results in poorer outcomes than if the work had never been done in the first place. Although your lead carpenter is skilled in overseeing a framing crew, is he or she prepared to oversee the project while you're away?

2. Assess the Order of Priorities

Take a step back and reconsider your priorities if they are being dictated by urgency. Something does not always need to be significant just because it is urgent.

The distinction may seem like a word trap, but the Eisenhower Principle simplifies it. According to this principle, urgent activities require immediate attention. They are typically connected to accomplishing the goals of others, while important activities have an outcome that leads to the achievement of personal and professional goals.

Setting priorities requires understanding the difference. Sort your jobs into one of the following categories on your to-do list to determine which definition they correspond with:

● Vital & Important

Crucial but Not Expedient

● Not Vital but Important ● Not Vital and Not Urgent

The first category will consist of chores you have avoided or haven't anticipated. Take care of things immediately, then set aside time each week or day to deal with these unforeseen circumstances. Give yourself enough time to do the second category of jobs so that you can perform them well, or assign them to someone else with extra caution so that the tasks don't become rework or emergency problems. The third type of job is likely one you can assign or reschedule, and the fourth category of tasks should be avoided as they are distractions.

3. Give Up Postponing

You may be able to rationalize procrastination to yourself and probably even your staff if you use the cynical yet appropriate phrase, "If it weren't for the last minute, nothing would get done." Still, it won't lessen the harm it causes. First of all, try not to punish yourself for putting off tasks. It's a common, although dishonest, behavior.

"Everyone puts things off sometimes, but procrastinators deliberately seek out distractions and avoid tasks regularly," states Psychology Today. Examine your reasons for procrastinating and your connection with it in depth. This is crucial because, as a chronic procrastinator, you negatively impact your business and all facets of your life.

You can train yourself to gradually take risks to overcome the tendency to selectively put off tasks. Acknowledge your accomplishments to yourself to gradually overcome your fear of success or failure. Some people put things off to escape, taking accountability for the result of their actions. For them, beating procrastination is accepting responsibility—even when it means admitting mistakes occasionally. While beating procrastination is a personal journey, successful time management depends on it.

4. Lessen Interruptions

There will be fewer distractions if you learn to prioritize and delegate, but there will still be plenty of people vying for your time and attention. The newest wave of diversions includes social media, email, texts, and a wealth of quickly accessed information on the internet. There are still some tried-and-true forms of distraction, such as pointless gatherings, inadequately designed processes, and busy work that can be mechanized.

Saying no is mostly the key to overcoming procrastination regarding technology. Refrain from opening your email every time you receive a notification. (Most emails can be answered within an hour, if not more, up to a day.) Avoid visiting your preferred automobile website for the latest new truck ratings.

To cut down on or completely eradicate the time wasters in the tried-and-true group, you need to delve a little further. Workflows frequently become unnecessary or out of date. Examine the daily actions you perform automatically, and you'll probably find several that you may modify or do away with entirely.

Observe the meetings you attend and pose some thought-provoking questions to yourself. Is this meeting set to happen again? Meetings that repeat frequently can be skipped. Are there goals and clear agendas for this meeting? How frequently are meetings rescheduled? Imagine the impact pointless and repetitive meetings have on the organization's productivity if they keep you from completing more critical tasks.

Automate tasks: thanks to modern technology, you can set routine chores to run on autopilot, freeing you and your staff to focus on more meaningful and appropriate work. Lastly, be sure you are establishing and upholding boundaries. Performing at your highest level is difficult when others believe you are easily distracted.

Setting Priorities And Making Plans

This chapter will cover the significance of planning and setting priorities to maximize output and make the most of our time. Time is money; therefore, if we don't prioritize our responsibilities and make time for them in our schedules, we risk squandering it on unimportant chores or letting crucial ones be overlooked.

Creating a to-do list is the first stage in planning and prioritizing. This list should contain every duty we have to finish, from the most crucial to the least crucial. Next, by placing the most crucial jobs at the top and the least crucial tasks at the bottom of the list, we may prioritize them. This ensures we don't squander time on low-priority chores and instead focus on the most important ones first.

Time-blocking is an essential component of planning and prioritization. This entails devoting particular time blocks to particular jobs or pursuits. For instance, we may set up a certain amount of time every day for checking and replying to emails and another set aside for finishing urgent work. Setting time blocks can ensure we don't become sidetracked from our work.

Recognizing our patterns and inclinations is critical to organizing and prioritizing tasks efficiently. While some people are most prolific in the afternoons or evenings, others are more productive in the mornings. By recognizing our natural rhythms, we can prevent squandering time during less productive times by scheduling our most critical work during our most productive hours.

Barack Obama, the former president, is a well-known example of planning and setting priorities. He had a reputation for keeping a rigorous schedule and exercising considerable self-control with his time. Every day, he would get up early to work out before reading and getting ready for meetings for the first few hours. Putting his health and intellectual development first in the morning allowed him to be more focused and productive the rest of the day.

Setting priorities and making a strategy are vital, as are being adaptive and flexible. Unforeseen circumstances and emergencies can derail our plans; therefore, we must be able to modify our schedules appropriately. We can deal with unforeseen events without compromising our productivity if we allow for some flexibility and leave buffer time between jobs.

Planning and setting priorities are essential for reaching our objectives and increasing productivity. We may manage our time and make the most of every minute by creating a to-do list, setting priorities, time-blocking, being aware of our rhythms, and maintaining flexibility. Time is money; therefore, we can invest in our futures and lead more satisfying lives by setting priorities and making plans.

Embracing New Paradigms and Solidifying Change

It's essential to embrace and accept change to overcome resistance and negativity. When everyone knows about the upcoming changes, there won't be any cause for dread. Given that humans are naturally flexible, it is your responsibility as a leader to encourage, uplift, and support your team members. Since outdated ideas and contemporary settings frequently collide, adjusting and implementing cutting-edge strategies for contemporary workplaces is critical.

Management Based Only on Results. The results-only management model is one such strategy that emphasizes worker production over presence. Because employees may select when, where, and how they work, this approach promotes trust and brings out the best in them, allowing them to concentrate on meeting goals rather than wasting time on menial activities.

For instance, a software company that adopted a results-only management approach greatly boosted productivity and employee happiness.

Workers valued freedom and flexibility, which improved output and eventually raised the company's earnings.

The Revolution in Wellbeing. The wellness revolution, which emphasizes the value of employees' physical and emotional well, is another contemporary workplace trend. Employers may empower their workers to have a better work-life balance by adopting decisions that prioritize the health of the entire workforce.

Prioritizing employee wellbeing can significantly impact a business, enhancing job satisfaction and productivity. For instance, a marketing company saw performance after implementing flexible scheduling, mental wellness days, and fitness programs.

Because these new models have different priorities and expectations from traditional methods, contemporary methods emphasize outcomes, flexibility, and wellbeing more than traditional methods, which emphasize presence and strict timetables.

In conclusion, to overcome resistance and adjust to the changing nature of the workplace, it is imperative that one embrace and accept change. Organizations and employees can benefit from a healthy work environment that firms cultivate by concentrating on employee wellness and implementing results-only management. It's time to move past outdated ideas and seize the opportunities the contemporary workplace presents.

Accepting Change and Succeeding in the Face of Uncertainty

Handling the Change Winds

Accepting change is the only way to move forward because it is unavoidable. However, how can one overcome resistance and embrace novel approaches to thinking and doing? The following tactics can assist you and your group in adjusting and prospering:

Sustain a Positive Attitude

It all starts with how you think about change. A positive outlook will motivate your team and assist you in overcoming obstacles. They are more inclined to trust and adhere to your advice if they perceive you as a self-assured leader receptive to fresh perspectives.

For example, the CEO of a well-known retail company had infectious joy and excitement as the company switched to e-commerce. The company's effective transformation was facilitated by the employees' motivation to acquire new skills and adjust to the demands of the digital marketplace.

Make Change Work for You: Examine how alterations may present fresh chances for development and advancement. If you have this mentality, you will see obstacles as chances to grow and achieve. For instance, a manufacturing company adopted automation and optimized its production process in response to heightened competition. They were able to concentrate on innovation and market expansion in addition to becoming more efficient due to this shift.

How to Use These Ideas and Techniques in Various Aspects of Your Life

You can use these ideas and tactics in various contexts, including employment, education, housing, health, hobbies, etc. To fit your requirements, tastes, or situation, you might need to modify them. Here are some instances of how you might use these ideas and techniques in various spheres of your life:

Work: You can assign or outsource part of your work to your team or outside partners, batch or automate some of your emails or reports, set SMART goals for your projects or plan for deadlines or meetings, and remove distractions from your desk or the internet.

● Study: You can batch or automate some of your notes or flashcards, set SMART goals for your classes or assignments, prioritize them based on their difficulty and due date, plan for your exams or presentations, assign or outsource some of your research or editing to your classmates or tutors, and remove distractions from your laptop or library.

● At home: You can automate or batch process some of your bills and subscriptions, remove distractions from your TV and phone, plan for your meals and grocery shopping, assign or outsource some of your cleaning and laundry to family members or services, and set SMART goals for your household chores and errands.

● Health: You may assign or outsource some of your cooking or tracking to friends or apps, batch or automate some of your supplements or reminders, set SMART goals for your fitness or wellness, prioritize them based on their advantages and enjoyment, schedule your workouts and appointments in advance, and get rid of distractions from your couch and snacks.

● Hobbies: You can batch or automate some of your learning or practice, set SMART goals for your hobbies or passions, prioritize them based on their enjoyment and fulfillment, plan for your sessions or events, assign or outsource some of your equipment or preparation to your mentors or clubs, and remove distractions from your job or family.

Here are some illustrations and case studies of how these ideas and tactics have helped successful individuals or businesses.

Numerous prosperous individuals or organizations across various sectors and domains have succeeded with these concepts and tactics. The following are some illustrations and case studies of how they have enhanced their productivity and time management by utilizing these ideas and techniques:

● Elon Musk is renowned for having lofty and imaginative ambitions. Using the SMART goal-setting method, he breaks down his large ambitions into smaller, more doable steps. For instance, he has broken down his 2024 target of colonizing Mars into multiple smaller objectives, such as launching the Starship rocket by 2020, completing the first crewed voyage by 2022, and building a permanent colony by 2024. He also applies the prioritization concept in numerous endeavors to concentrate on the most crucial and pressing duties.

He adheres to a daily calendar that allows time for meetings, emails, calls, engineering, design, and other tasks based on priority. He also groups related chores together and completes them all simultaneously using batching. He commits, for instance, to SpaceX on Mondays and Fridays, Tesla on Tuesdays and Thursdays, and his other initiatives on Wednesdays. To eliminate distractions from his workspace, he also applies the elimination principle. He works in a calm, uncluttered office without windows, décor, or a phone. In addition, he avoids pointless meetings and uses social media in moderation.

● Oprah Winfrey: The philanthropist and media magnate is well-known for her influence and output. She prepares for her responsibilities and objectives by adhering to the planning ahead principle. She has a morning routine that involves reading, writing in her gratitude diary, exercising, and meditation. She arranges her daily agenda and responsibilities using a planner as well. She also assigns some of her tasks to her partners or team members using delegation.

She is assisted in her media production, company administration, charitable activities, etc., by a team of reliable employees. She also streamlines some of her systems and procedures using the automation approach. She uses software and technology to handle marketing, communications, banking, and other tasks. She also applies the elimination principle to eliminate distractions in both her personal and work lives. She stays away from gossiping, reading bad news, and watching TV. In addition, she establishes boundaries with people and declines invitations and requests that conflict with her principles or aspirations.

- Amazon: Known for its efficiency and ingenuity, this e-commerce behemoth is also a leader in technology. It establishes specific, attainable goals for its goods and services using the SMART goal-setting technique. It aligns its objectives with its vision and mission using the OKR (Objectives and Key Results) framework. To concentrate on the most crucial and pressing tasks for its stakeholders and customers, it also applies the prioritization approach. It prioritizes the consumer's needs in all that it does by adhering to the customer obsession philosophy. Additionally, it employs the two-pizza rule to keep team sizes to a maximum of ten members, which lowers the expense of coordination and communication. It also applies the idea of planning to foresee future trends and possibilities. It aims to outperform its rivals by ten times using the 10x rule. It also uses the six-page memo technique, simplifying and condensing complex ideas. It also allows its partners and staff to decide and take the initiative by applying the delegating principle.

By implementing the ownership principle, it holds its staff members responsible for their actions and results. It also groups related jobs together and completes them all at once using the batching principle. It streamlines the online purchasing experience for its clients by utilizing the one-click ordering capability. It also automates several of its systems and procedures using the automation principle. To improve its operations, delivery, customer service, etc., it uses robotics, cloud computing, artificial intelligence, machine learning, etc. It also applies the elimination principle to eliminate waste and inefficiency from its value chain. Applying the lean management concept eliminates any activity that does not provide value to its stakeholders or consumers.

Conventional Instruments For Monitoring Goals

Using conventional goal-tracking methods may seem outdated in this digital world. However, these technologies have shown their value over time and often offer an alternative but functional viewpoint on time management. These conventional tools include the goal diary, calendar, to-do list, and token system.

To begin with, a to-do list is arguably one of the simplest yet most effective tools for tracking goals. Putting your to-do list in writing will help you focus on finishing the activities rather than worrying about remembering them all. A to-do list, however, serves as more than just a basic reminder—it also helps us prioritize and plan out our responsibilities.

It's crucial to have a to-do list that is practical and concise. Don't give yourself too many impossible jobs or obstacles to overcome. Rather, attempt to divide ambitious objectives into smaller, more doable activities. Using "task breakdown," you can move closer to your larger objectives without feeling overburdened.

The calendar is yet another essential tool from the past for managing your schedule. A calendar lets you plan and keep track of your long-term objectives, while a to-do list is better used for tracking short-term chores. A calendar helps you see how your obligations are divided and when you will have spare time by displaying your chores and commitments throughout time.

Using a calendar can also prevent job overload and identify scheduling issues. Planning long-term projects, where multiple tasks could need your attention at once, is where this is very helpful. By planning items on your calendar, you can ensure adequate time for each task and prevent last-minute stress.

Your goal diary can be an effective tool for goal tracking, in addition to your calendar and to-do list. This tool emphasizes introspection and self-evaluation more than other tools. You may monitor your development, spot trends and issues, and remember your experiences and lessons by keeping a goal journal.

It's not necessary to have a complicated goal journal. It can be as easy as jotting down your daily accomplishments, obstacles you've encountered, and solutions. Nevertheless, even if it seems straightforward, keeping a goal journal can teach you a lot about working when you are most productive and managing your time better.

Finally, a tool that combines calendar items and to-do lists is the tab system. This method, made popular by American television writer and producer Ryan Holiday, entails writing objectives or tasks on separate index cards, which are then arranged logically.

Every tab denotes a task or objective and can be arranged in many categories or order as required. This technique is especially helpful for long-term projects or jobs that must be completed in a certain order.

In summary, conventional tools are still useful for goal tracking and time management, even though they could appear basic compared to contemporary digital apps and programs. You can utilize the to-do list, calendar, goal journal, and tab system to increase productivity, maintain focus on your objectives, and enhance time management. Always keep in mind that the ideal tool is the one that can adjust most effectively.

Section Five

Establishing Productive Time Management Routines

cultivating motivation and self-control

Self-control and motivation are

necessary for developing effective time management techniques. To cultivate discipline, set clear expectations, and take responsibility for your actions. Make a timetable and follow it despite outside distractions or temptations. Try self-motivation techniques that resonate with you, such as envisioning the advantages of reaching your objectives or reminding yourself of the negative effects of poor time management. You may stay committed to efficient time management by becoming more self-motivated and disciplined.

Overcoming Perfectionism and Analytical Paralysis

Perfectionism and paralysis by analysis may be impeding your efforts to manage your time. Aim high, but recognize that greatness is often unattainable and might lead to wasting time on little things. Acquire the capacity to prioritize tasks and make judgments with efficiency. Recognize that learning is a process that involves errors and imperfections and set appropriate expectations. To prevent analysis paralysis, set time limits for decision-making and focus on gathering the essential information to make informed choices. By getting over your perfectionism and analytical paralysis, you can enhance your time management and avoid getting sucked into unproductive loops.

Make a timetable with activities to energize you and help you prepare for the day. Start with activities that enhance your physical and mental wellbeing, such as yoga, meditation, or journaling. Set priorities, evaluate your objectives, and schedule your day.

utilizing effective time management strategies during breaks and idle periods Being able to manage your time well outside of the office is beneficial. Make thoughtful use of downtime and breaks to refresh and increase productivity. Use the little breaks between tasks to relax, stretch, or engage in a quick, refreshing activity. During lengthier breaks, partake in activities that promote rest or personal development.

Or leisure activities like hobbies, reading, or spending time with loved ones. Avoid using excessive amounts of energy on screens or energy-draining hobbies. Using wise time management strategies during breaks and downtime can boost your total productivity and preserve a healthy work-life balance.

Establishing effective time management skills is a continuous process that requires dedication and perseverance. Creating a morning routine, overcoming analytical paralysis and perfectionism, and growing in self-discipline and determination.

1.5 Reevaluating and Modifying Your Objectives

Our priorities shift with the times, as do our lives. To make the most of your time and keep your attention on what is important, it is imperative that you periodically review and modify your priorities. To assist you in reevaluating and reordering your priorities, consider these steps:

1. Think back on your objectives: Set aside some time to review your short- and long-term objectives. Assess whether they still fit your goals, values, and situation. Modify your objectives if needed to better align them with your present priorities.

2. Analyze your progress: Assess the success of your present prioritization techniques and your progress toward your goals. Determine any barriers or difficulties that impede your development and consider ways to overcome them.

3. Determine what has changed in your life: Think about any major life changes that have taken place, including a new job, a change in family situation, or more obligations. Your priorities might need to change as a result of these adjustments.

4. Reorder tasks: Using strategies like the Eisenhower Matrix or the ABCDE method, rearrange your tasks in order of

importance based on your analysis and reflection. Your to-do list should be updated to reflect your changed priorities.

5. As you reevaluate your priorities, you might discover that some duties are no longer necessary or can be assigned to someone else. Assign or do away with these duties to make more time for higher-priority work.

6. Reevaluate your priorities and make necessary schedule adjustments to make room for new assignments or to give high-priority activities more time. Ensure that your time blocks, calendar, and daily schedule all match your revised priorities.

7. Remain adaptable: Recognize that your priorities could shift over time, and be ready to make adjustments as necessary. It takes flexibility and adaptability to manage your time well and keep a good work-life balance.

Making the most of your time and focusing on what is important requires you to regularly review and revise your priorities. Time management techniques stay useful and consistent with your objectives and morals.

Chapter 2: Make SMART Objectives

2.1 The Influence of Objectives

Setting goals is an effective strategy for maintaining motivation, focus, and progress toward your objectives. By defining your goals precisely, you may make a successful plan to lead you through the actions required to accomplish your goals. Setting goals has the following benefits that give it power:

1. Give you direction: Your goals serve as a compass to assist you in getting through all of the responsibilities and distractions that life throws you. You can choose where to spend your time and energy more wisely if you know what you want to accomplish.

2. Boost focus: It's simpler when you have specific objectives. With this enhanced focus, you may be more productive and progress toward your goals.

3. Boost motivation: You'll be more motivated to strive toward your objectives if you set difficult but doable ones. Accomplishing a goal may further fuel your urge to pursue new objectives.

4. Promote personal development: Setting goals forces you to venture outside your comfort zone and work for development and betterment. You will learn new things, get new experiences, and gain new insights into yourself as you strive for your objectives.

5. Promote prioritization: Setting priorities for your duties and obligations is simpler by having well-defined goals. You may manage your time and resources more efficiently by knowing

which tasks will help you reach your objectives.

6. Encourage a feeling of purpose: Setting goals gives you a reason to get out of bed in the morning and face the day ahead. They also give you a sense of meaning and purpose. Achieving objectives per your principles can improve your general happiness and wellbeing.

For wellbeing, consider SMART goals and how to set and meet them successfully in the upcoming sub-chapters to enhance productivity and time management.

Multitasking in Chapter 6

M

Multitasking is the act of completing several tasks at once. Even though it could appear to promote productivity, it might result in less efficiency and more stress. This chapter will address the benefits and drawbacks of multitasking and offer effective methods for handling several things simultaneously.

The ability to work on several tasks at once is known as multitasking. It can help you do more tasks in less time, so it is frequently regarded as a desired talent. But, multitasking can often get in the way of efficient time management. Here are some pointers to help you better manage your time and multitask:

Set task priorities: To multitask effectively, tasks must be prioritized. Prioritize the things on your list according to their urgency and significance. This enables you to effectively multitask and concentrate on the most crucial tasks.

Combine related tasks: Combining related tasks can help you multitask more effectively. For instance, if you must make phone calls, set out a specific period to make all your calls simultaneously. You can stay focused and finish work more quickly as a result.

Use technology: Increasing the effectiveness of multitasking can be achieved with the help of technology. Use productivity tools like task management software to stay organized and effectively manage your responsibilities. While completing other duties, stay in touch with clients and coworkers via email and instant messaging.

Refrain from distractions: They can drastically lower the effectiveness of multitasking. Determine the typical sources of distraction and make every effort to minimize or remove them. This may include deleting pointless tabs on your computer, disabling your phone's notifications, or finding a quiet workplace.

Recognize your boundaries: When it comes to multitasking, it's critical to recognize your boundaries. Attempting to multitask excessively increases the likelihood of errors and decreases productivity. Regarding how much you can do at once, be practical and don't put too much on your plate.

Take breaks: Increasing the effectiveness of your multitasking requires taking breaks. You can reenergize and refocus, which increases your effectiveness and productivity.

Make sure you plan regular pause times during the day so that you can recuperate, unwind, and rejuvenate.

Acquire the skill of effectively switching between tasks: Successful multitasking requires effective task switching. Ensure you finish a task before going on to the next one, and try not to jump between duties too often. You can stay focused and finish work more quickly as a result.

To sum up, multitasking can be an effective strategy for increasing time management effectiveness, but it needs to be well planned and carried out. You may increase your multitasking efficiency and accomplish your goals more successfully by prioritizing work, grouping related tasks, using technology, avoiding distractions, understanding your limits, taking breaks, and switching tasks effectively. To ensure your tactics align with your current priorities and objectives, don't forget to examine and tweak them frequently.

The following section will discuss the value of task delegation and efficient task delegation.

Postpone Making a Decision

Making decisions can be stressful, which can lead to procrastination. People often put off making decisions when presented with difficult options or novel jobs because they fear choosing the incorrect option. Decision delay is the term for this kind of delay, where people put off making decisions to prevent unfavorable outcomes. The need to feel in control of the outcome is the root cause of decision delay. However, when crucial decisions are postponed or avoided completely, this propensity can result in lost chances and untapped potential.

Substitute Award

When people swap out an internal task reward for an external incentive or reward, this is known as reward substitution. For instance, a student may put off preparing for an exam until the very last minute, hoping that the stress of a deadline will instill a sense of enthusiasm and urgency in him. This external pressure momentarily replaces the natural satisfaction of mastering the content. Reward replacement prolongs a cycle of depending on outside triggers to start action, even when it can result in a last-minute productivity boost. Developing an inherent motivation that surpasses the desire for outside benefits is difficult.

The Fallacy of Planning

A cognitive bias known as planning error occurs when people underestimate the time, money, and effort needed to do a task. Because people tend to overestimate their ability to finish activities more quickly than they can, this overly optimistic assessment can result in poor time management. Consequently, individuals could put off beginning assignments, thinking they have ample time to finish the work alone as the due date draws near. Lack of knowledge or experience with the current task frequently worsens scheduling problems. Implementing time management techniques and gaining a more precise understanding of task requirements are necessary to overcome this bias.

In brief

Procrastination is influenced by a variety of psychological factors that are intricately linked to human nature. These elements offer important insights into the fundamental causes of human procrastination, ranging from the fear of failure and self-doubt that impair our talents to the desire for fast pleasure and the biases that influence our decision-making.

It is essential to identify and comprehend these psychological aspects to overcome procrastination. We can start to break out of the web of entrapment by confronting our concerns, increasing our self-efficacy, and creating plans to resist the temptations of rapid pleasure. In the ensuing chapters, we will delve into methods for surmounting these mental obstacles, equipping us to break free from the hold of procrastination and clearing the path for ongoing development and productivity.

Tenacity To Dispel Myths

Even though it was aware of its limits compared to the hare, the tortoise had questioned the superiority of speed. This calls for bravery and tenacity. Everywhere we look in daily life, we encounter people bragging. It is wise to ignore them for the most part, but when they become intolerable, they must be confronted. A simple inquiry, thud, or admonition might sometimes be enough to check someone. There are occasions when confronting is necessary in addition to simple inquiry. It can be a coworker who frequently sarcastically disparages you. Often, a polite reprimand will make them stop. It's time to address them if not. Being compassionate to others is wonderful, but it shouldn't be viewed as a sign of weakness.

c. Death by procrastination

Just as smoking is exhilarating but deadly, procrastinating is also exhilarating but deadly. Our wonderful hare put things off and rested, and in the end, the hardworking tortoise got its chance.

Failure to plan is the Death of success.

Barbara Oakley

Books addressing the topic of beating procrastination abound. It's the stuff that destroys careers and causes family strife, among other things. One thing to remember is that life is brief, and we should prioritize completing the most crucial tasks. It turns out that the hardest and simplest chore to put off is also the most crucial one. We waste time in lengthy, pointless meetings and lose sight of why we were employed. Try your hardest and most challenging task first.

According to a quote by Mark Twain, if you eat a live frog first thing in the morning.

Brian Tracy (d).

Even while it may sound cliche, the fact nevertheless stands. The competition between Captain Scot and Amundsen to reach the South Pole serves as another illustration of this. This is demonstrated in an extract from Jim Collin's book, Great By Choice.

Two expeditions set out to become the first persons in modern history to reach the South Pole, and in October 1911, they completed their last preparations. There were two expedition leaders with comparable experience and ages (39 and 43): Roald Amundsen, the winner, and Robert Falcon Scott, the loser. Within days of one another, Amundsen and Scott set off on their separate expeditions to reach the Pole. They faced an unknown and harsh climate, with temperatures that might drop as low as 20° below zero even in the summer, compounded worse by gale-force winds.

Their combined trips would take them more than 1,400 miles round trip.

Amundsen followed a strict program of constant advancement during the expedition, never traveling too far in favorable conditions, being cautious to avoid the red line of fatigue that may expose his team, and pushing through inclement weather to maintain his pace. Amundsen reduced the daily mileage of his skilled group to 15–20 miles as they marched relentlessly southward towards 90°. On poor days, on the other hand, Scott would occasionally sit in his tent and whine about the weather after pushing his squad to the brink of fatigue on good days. Amundsen reached the South Pole precisely on schedule, averaging fifteen and a half miles each Day.

The abovementioned situation seems like the tale of the tortoise and the hare. Life is a marathon, and those who are patient and persistent win races (marathons, not sprints).

Hasty climbers fall off suddenly.

A quick runner will not last very long.

Step 7: Hiring Helpers

While breaking harmful habits is never simple, it can be made a lot simpler with the help of friends and family. The people in your life have the power to offer responsibility and support, both of which are crucial while attempting to break a habit. As you take on this endeavor, contact them if you need assistance or even some moral support.

Locating a group of like-minded people who share your goals on the internet can also be helpful. This can help you feel friendship and remind you that you're not traveling alone.

Connecting with people who are aware of your struggles can be quite beneficial for maintaining motivation and focus.

Tell your loved ones about your objectives and solicit their assistance. They can support you and hold you responsible.

Additionally, consider consulting with a time management or ADHD-focused coach or therapist. They may offer you tailored guidance and assist you in developing efficient time management techniques.

Joining an online forum or support group with others who face comparable difficulties could also be beneficial. It can be immensely empowering to connect with those who have similar struggles with tardiness behaviors. Having a confidant with whom to share tales, discuss, and receive advice can be beneficial.

Whatever you do, remember that it's a process that calls for perseverance and commitment. It takes time to break the habit of being late, but you can succeed if you have the correct support system and methods! Wishing you luck!

Practice: Tracking Tick Tock

This is a useful activity that can help people with ADHD become more adept at managing their time:

1. Be realistic in your task estimates, but remember that you may overestimate or underestimate the time needed.

2. Track how long it takes to finish each job using a stopwatch or timer.

3. Examine any discrepancies between your estimated and actual times and consider potential causes.

4. Decide on at least one tactic to improve your time management and estimation going forward.

5. Use this method for your next projects and track productivity and time management gains.

Here's an illustration to help you grasp it better:

Today's assignments include completing a work report and tidying the bedroom.

Put each assignment in writing along with an estimated time of completion.

● Spend 30 minutes cleaning your bedroom.

Completing a job report takes one hour.

Use a stopwatch or timer to keep track of how long each task takes.

● Spend 45 minutes cleaning your bedroom.

Completing a work report took one hour and fifteen minutes.

Take note of any discrepancies between your estimated and actual times.

You realize halfway through that cleaning your bedroom took longer than anticipated since you got distracted organizing your wardrobe.

● Due to the need for further research, completing the work report took longer than anticipated.

Choose at least one tactic that will assist you in the future in more accurately estimating and managing your time.

● Divide cleaning duties into smaller sections and assign specified times for each phase. ● You could provide extra time for job assignments to research in case of unforeseen challenges.

Use this method for your upcoming responsibilities to see whether it helps you be more productive and manage your time better. You may, for instance, divide cleaning your kitchen into manageable steps (such as washing dishes, wiping down counters, and sweeping) and assign specified times to each task.

Remember, this exercise aims to help you discover the most effective tactics for you and obtain insight into your sense of time and routines. It's okay if you need to experiment a little to figure out what works; what matters is that you're taking the initiative to improve how you manage your time.

Developing Concentration

Picture yourself in a comfortable, well-lit office with motivational wall sayings and pleasant colors. You take a brief pause to stretch and practice deep breathing. When you return to your job, you feel renewed and invigorated. You're feeling motivated and determined because of the positive atmosphere surrounding you.

Creating a cozy and pleasant environment is one of the finest methods for controlling distractions. This can be as simple as arranging happy-making objects and colors around your workspace, like plants or family photos. You could be more motivated to stay focused and finish things if your workstation is a place you enjoy spending time in.

Adding exercise and movement to your Day is another way to help you deal with distractions. Frequent exercise helps enhance focus and lower tension, making controlling distractions simpler. Think about taking a little stroll or performing stretches during your job breaks. This will not only assist you in maintaining attention, but it will also enhance your general well-being.

Taking breaks and giving your brain a mental recharge throughout the Day is also critical. When you return to work after allowing your brain to recover and rejuvenate, you might be more efficient and adept at handling interruptions. This could be taking a quick nap, engaging in mindfulness exercises, or taking a brief break from work.

Similar to a computer, Just like an excessive number of open applications on a computer might cause it to lag and consume more RAM, an excessive number of ideas and tasks in your head can also lower your mental and physical output. You can relax and rejuvenate yourself by pausing and engaging in mindfulness exercises. Putting these methods and approaches into practice allows you to become more focused and lead the fulfilling life you've always wanted.

Practice: Day-Theming

Day Theming is a method that entails putting related work in groups and allocating them to particular days of the week. Those with ADHD who have trouble focusing and staying organized can benefit from this strategy. You can minimize distractions from switching between different sorts of work and prevent decision fatigue by designating specific days for specific duties.

The following are some pointers for using Day Theming:

● Begin by listing what you typically have to accomplish for your job or personal life.

● Assign each task to a particular day of the week according to your workload and preferences.

● Be adaptable and modify your plans in response to unforeseen circumstances or shift priorities.

● To stay consistent and follow your routine, use a planner or calendar.

You may lower daily stress and boost productivity by practicing Day Theming. Maintaining a schedule will make it simpler for you to concentrate on the current duties and reduce your likelihood of putting them off or feeling overburdened by your job.

You can schedule leisure activities and self-care by using day theming. Your timetable can be more flexible by allocating particular days for particular responsibilities, leaving time for hobbies and leisure.

Determine when you are most productive during the Day and plan to complete critical activities then.

Knowing your biological cycles or chronotypes can greatly help your quest for productivity. Everybody has an internal body clock called the circadian rhythm, which controls various physiological functions such as hormone production, mood swings, and sleep-wake cycles. Influenced by your chronotype, which has an impact on your productivity. You may maximize your productivity and work more efficiently by determining when you are most productive during the Day and scheduling critical chores accordingly.

Productivity gurus have coined the term "biological prime time" to describe the window of time when your mood, energy, and concentration are at their highest. This usually falls within a timeframe of two to four hours. But depending on the individual, this window may open differently. Some folks, sometimes called "morning larks," discover that they are most focused and awake in the morning. Some people, referred to as "night owls," are most productive in the evenings. Additionally, a subset of persons referred to as "afternoon people" reach their peak in the early afternoon.

Determining your biological prime time entails tracking your energy and concentration levels over a day. Certain patterns might become apparent, such as feeling lethargic after lunch but getting a second wind in the late afternoon. You might use productivity tools to track your work habits or just keep a basic journal where you record your energy levels every hour. You'll eventually notice a trend that helps direct your task schedule.

The next step is to set aside this time for your most difficult and critical tasks—those that call for the greatest amount of cognitive capacity—after determining when you're most effective during the Day. These could be creative, strategic thinking, or problem-solving exercises. You can be certain that you're giving the most important parts of your work your best effort by scheduling these chores when you're most productive.

On the other hand, you can set aside time for less difficult or lower-priority duties, including meetings, administrative work, or regular housekeeping, during periods when your energy tends to decline. By doing this, you're maximizing your energy fluctuations rather than attempting to resist them throughout the Day.

Apart from synchronizing your work schedule with your internal clock, you can employ techniques to amplify your energy and concentration during your moments of maximum production. These could include avoiding unnecessary distractions, taking quick breaks to recharge, and eating and drinking sensibly.

It's crucial to remember that your chronotype may alter over your life due to various factors, including age and lifestyle modifications. As a result, it's helpful to review your most productive periods from time to time and modify your plan accordingly.

Furthermore, even if knowing your chronotype and setting activities in line with it can greatly increase productivity, it's not always possible because of outside factors like work schedules, family obligations, or social conventions. It's critical to discover alternative energy and concentration management strategies in these situations, such as adhering to a normal sleep schedule, engaging in mindfulness exercises, and taking regular pauses.

In conclusion, one effective tactic for increasing productivity is determining when you are most productive during the Day and planning critical chores around that time. It's about synchronizing your movements with your body's inherent rhythms instead of fighting them. You can set up your work schedule to maximize productivity and promote general well-being by being aware of and mindful of your biological rhythm.

The Significance Of Proficient Time Management.

● It could help in meeting deadlines

Not only are deadlines and appointments difficult to remember but they can easily be overlooked if one is not careful.

Using calendars and other tools to better organize your time will probably be helpful if you struggle to do so yourself. An organization that barely reaches its goals may find that effective time management is crucial. Keeping all your appointments and due dates in one place facilitates more effective time management.

Effective time management has the potential to improve focus and productivity.

Learning how to manage your time effectively and when and how to focus your efforts are key components of time management, which goes beyond just adding more tasks to your list. As a result, most business owners will see an increase in production and an improvement in their company's efficiency, which is always advantageous.

● Less procrastination may result from better time management.

Likewise, most will discover that implementing better time management practices at work will often help to lessen procrastination. You'll be less distracted, and everyone can finish the job sooner if you and your team focus more on the current task.

Concentrating when you are working under a set schedule with duties assigned to particular time slots throughout the day will be simpler. This is because you will be aware that each task has a deadline that you must meet.

Consequently, you won't put off working on such duties as much. As a result, you'll acquire more effective procrastination management skills.

● A well-planned schedule can result in greater freedom and less stress.

It's stressful to race against the clock to meet a deadline since you never know if you'll succeed. However, having good time management skills lets you view your workday as a series of tasks that you must complete rather than a whole.

It is simple to prioritize your tasks and establish plans to ensure you don't experience too much stress once you have organized your responsibilities and know exactly when to complete them.

Others might be surprised to learn that managing your time will often be much more liberating and reduce stress at work. You'll frequently be able to achieve a better work-life balance when you set out time for specific tasks or projects and are aware of what has to be accomplished.

● It maintains your standing in the workplace.

If you give lousy time management enough time, it will damage your reputation. Other consequences of poor time management include missing deadlines, rushing assignments, and skipping meetings.

Effective time management, however, eliminates these chances and aids in building and maintaining your professional reputation.

● It also helps avoid expensive fines.

Your business involves more than just meeting project deadlines; for instance, you must ensure that taxes are paid on schedule. Your return is late unless you wish to pay an additional 5% fee each month.

You'll stay out of trouble if you set up a specific period on your calendar for handling taxes and other expenses in your business.

● Effective time management could help achieve a better work-life balance.

When you manage your time well, you will create a formal schedule for your days.

Additionally, you'll be well on your way to creating a clear work-life balance when you track how your day is divided between professional and personal responsibilities. one that guarantees you'll have time for both.

CHAPTER 3: SETTING SMART, VISIBLE GOALS

Setting goals at an organization can be challenging, particularly if many people are working there for whom the goals need to be specified. With the greatest of intentions, these goals are often formulated and articulated, but little happens after the initial thrill. Well-aligned goals can provide direction for both companies and their employees. Establishing objectives helps people and organizations understand their purpose and makes it simpler for them to figure out how to follow suit.

What is goal setting exactly?

Establishing objectives can be done on an individual, team, or corporate basis. Establishing objectives means reaching a goal in any form within a given time frame. Individual objectives could be as simple as organizational goals and lofty as "changing how society perceives a certain problem."

Which four objectives make up the core of goal setting?

Setting goals yields four important outcomes: accountability, motivation, vision, and fulfillment (or achievement). These findings support employees in understanding their place in the larger vision, working towards it, and joining the team in celebration when the goal is accomplished.

principal objectives of goal-setting

1. Increasing drive

Establishing objectives could motivate employees to take on projects outside their comfort zones. Employee engagement is higher when they have a goal to strive for, and studies show that goal-setting strengthens workers' sense of commitment to their employer. This boosts workplace morale and motivates workers to perform better.

2. Pursuing a shared objective

If very intelligent individuals working on the same project produce radically different results, the problem is a lack of a shared vision. By setting global and micro goals, managers can determine when providing feedback is critical.

3. Taking on more accountability

Setting goals helps keep employees responsible. The next stage after creating goals is to evaluate their progress. This way of thinking also benefits managers in remote work by empowering them to challenge employees directly about meeting goals, performance, or anything else relevant.

4. Reaching predetermined goals

Creating goals is the most straightforward and trustworthy way to assess when a project is finished. Remote workers can concentrate on the objectives that clearly define success since they can concentrate on the output that must be provided by the deadline rather than worrying about completing their needed hours. Reaching objectives can increase employees' sense of fulfillment and overall job satisfaction and retention. Employees will probably feel more valued if they can track the strategy's development. This increased loyalty leads to higher retention rates.

www.ingramcontent.com/pod-product-compliance
Lightning Source LLC
Chambersburg PA
CBHW052139110526
44591CB00012B/1787